What's ours is Yours.

Welcome to the Polish cuisine!

THE BEST OF POLISH CUISINE

in Krakow

MEDIA PATRONAGE

RADIO KRAKÓW

Małopolska

Special thanks to
the Artistic Handicraft Cooperative Artistic Ceramics and Pottery
in Bolesławiec
for allowing to present our dishes on their pottery.

Text and Idea by Agnieszka Kozłowska & Wydawnictwo Kropka
Translated from Polish by Ewa Basiura, Helen Down,
INTER LANG & TEXT Kraków
Recepies, photographs and presentation by Wydawnictwo Kropka
Cover photograph by Paweł Mazur

ISBN 978-83-89975-23-2

Published by Wydawnictwo Kropka
Skr. pocztowa 125
65-901 Zielona Góra
tel. (+48 68) 321-15-72
www.ciastanastol.home.pl
ciastanastol@home.pl

Printed by Olsztyńskie Zakłady Graficzne
tel. (+48 89) 533-43-80

*Welcome to the hospitable city of Krakow with its special cuisine.
Experienced tourists know that nothing gives a better insight into
a foreign country and its culture than familiarity with its best-loved
national dishes and the ways in which they are prepared and served.
If the saying "tell me what you eat and I will tell you who you are"
is true, it offers a special context for culinary knowledge.
Polish cuisine is exceptionally rich. We, however, have selected the
most basic dishes that reflect its character and special taste. We focus
on their history and preparation, but also on those places in Krakow
where, in our opinion, you can eat the best Polish food.
Here you can find recipes for our most popular national dishes
presented in a simple and clear manner that guarantees culinary
success even to those who are novices in the kitchen.
On your return home, it will certainly be nice to delight your guests
with a Polish meal or to contribute to a special atmosphere by serving
a Polish dish while showing the pictures
or films from your trip to Poland.
We wish you unforgettable experiences at Polish tables
and a lot of fun while making dishes with our recipes.
We guarantee you success!
Enjoy your meals!*

Some comments on Polish cuisine

Polish cuisine, like the cuisine of other countries, has its own special taste. It traditionally uses staple elements which include meat, meat and vegetable stock, sour cream and animal fats. Also some dishes eaten in Poland on a daily basis are made from ingredients that do not always enjoy such popularity in other countries. These include mushrooms, gherkins and sauerkraut.

In traditional Polish households, four meals are served during the day – breakfast at about. 7.00 a.m., elevenses at noon, lunch between 3.00 p.m. and 4.00 p.m. (this is the main meal of the day) and dinner at around 8.00 p.m.

Of course, the present pace of life results in changes in meal times or even in skipping some of them. Also modern families are giving up the daily ritual in favour of culinary habits borrowed from abroad. Naturally, in this publication we are going to stick to traditional Polish cuisine.

The first two meals of the day are usually served cold, except for some egg dishes and milk soups. These meals may consist of cold cuts, cold roast meats, cheese, eggs or fish served with bread and butter. The most important meal is lunch, which comprises a soup, a main course and a dessert, which is frequently a kind of fruit drink. Dinner, the evening meal, consists of sandwiches or hot dishes that are simple and quick to make.

Since time immemorial Polish cuisine has been very sumptuous. The proverbial "old Polish hospitality", so well known all over the world, involved the obligation to feed well the guests crossing one's threshold. Often in the households of the Polish gentry breakfast would last until dinner or even longer. The dishes served included meats in heavy sauces, game and poultry, fish and dairy products. All these were accompanied by large quantities of alcohol, which considerably stimulated digestion. Some elements of these old customs are still alive in Poland, since no respectable hostess will allow guests to leave her home before their stomachs are fully replete. However, more sensible and reasonable hosts have given up insisting that their guests should eat as much as possible. Nevertheless, during more solemn meetings there is a definite superfluity of food at the Polish table.

In this book we present the most popular Polish dishes and we wish you some truly unforgettable experiences with them.

CHICKEN NOODLE SOUP

Rosół z makaronem

1 whole chicken, 2-3 carrots, 1 parsnip, half a medium celeriac, 1 leek, piece of white or Savoy cabbage, 1 onion, salt, several black peppercorns, soup seasoning, parsley to garnish.

This soup is served for dinner on Sundays, holidays, as well as at greater family gatherings, such as wedding, christening or first communion receptions. It tastes best when served with home-made noodles and there are many women in Poland who cannot imagine serving it with anything else. To produce a really delicious broth several different kinds of meat should be used.

1 Rinse the chicken well, place in cold water and bring almost to the boil.

2 When foam starts appearing on the surface it should be skimmed before the soup starts boiling, as the consistency should be clear.

3 When it starts boiling reduce to the lowest heat and cook for about an hour and a half; in the meantime add washed and diced soup vegetables and season with salt and black pepper.

4 Halve the onion and brown it on a hotplate or over a gas burner; add it to the broth.

5 Remove the meat and vegetables when tender.

Serve with noodles, rice or drop dumplings, lavishly sprinkled with finely chopped parsley.

NOODLES: *1.1 lb flour, 2 eggs, several spoonfuls of water, 1 tsp salt.*

1 Combine all the ingredients on a kneading board to make a rather stiff dough. Knead very well.

2 Roll out the dough thinly into several batches and then cut into fine vermicelli. Arrange a thin layer of noodles on the board and allow them to dry.

3 Cook in salted boiling water (7 pints) for three minutes after they have floated to the surface.

4 Drain the cooked noodles with a colander, rinse with cold water and drain well again.

SOUR CUCUMBER SOUP   *Ogórkowa*

11 oz pork or beef on the bone, 0.5 lb pickled cucumbers (large gherkins), 5 potatoes, 2 carrots, 1 parsnip, half a celeriac, 1 leek, 1 onion, dill, salt, black pepper, soup seasoning.

1 Rinse the meat, place in cold water (approx 6 glasses) and bring to the boil over a high heat. Then reduce the heat to low and simmer for about one hour.

2 Peel, rinse and dice the vegetables (grate the carrots coarsely). Peel and chop the onions. Put the vegetables into the parboiled vegetable stock and cook adding salt and pepper to taste.

3 When the meat and vegetables are tender drain them off, cut finely and put back into the soup (vegetables do not need to be put back).

4 Peel and dice the potatoes, put them into the soup and continue to simmer.

5 Peel the cucumber, grate coarsely and add to the soup when the potatoes are almost tender.

6 At the end add chopped dill and season to taste.

If you like you may add some sour cream.

*T*his soup is sour, but the large amount of vegetables and cream make its taste milder. The chopped or grated gherkins can be added together with the water in which they were marinated. This marinade is sometimes treated as a drink, since it really has a nice, refreshing taste. Of course, each housewife has her own cucumber soup recipe. It has to be emphasized that it is the most homely of all soups. It is usually prepared on an everyday basis, not for special occasions.

CABBAGE SOUP

Kapuśniak

1 lb sauerkraut or half a white cabbage (shredded), piece of bone, 1 lb pork, 3 oz streaky bacon or pork fat, several potatoes, 2-3 carrots, 1 leek, 1 celeriac, 1 parsnip, 1 onion, 1-2 dried mushrooms (if liked), 2 bay leaves, 4 grains of allspice, salt, black pepper, soup seasoning.

1 Put the sauerkraut or cabbage into a pot with 3 pints of water.

2 Add the bones, pork, carrots, parsnip, leek, celeriac, half the onion, bay leaves and allspice and dried mushrooms if used.

3 When the meat is cooked remove it and cut into fine pieces; chop the mushrooms.

4 Peel and dice the potatoes, put them into the soup and cook.

5 Dice the pork fat finely and fry until golden with half the chopped onion and a spoonful of flour. Add a little bit of the cabbage soup into this roux and stir well. Then pour into the soup and bring to the boil.

If the soup is made with sauerkraut you can make its taste milder by adding a teaspoonful of sugar. If it is made with fresh cabbage add a dash of vinegar and sugar.

This is yet another Polish sour soup, since Polish people love such tastes. The soup is quite thick and it can be made with vegetables and bacon or with fried pork fat or with meat. A particularly popular version is made in the Podhale region, where mutton on the bone forms the main ingredient. It is cooked in sauerkraut until tender. However, dishes made with acidic ingredients take very long to cook, so before the meat is tender the soup acquires a special, intensive taste. It is served with mushrooms and potatoes which should be cooked separately. The cabbage soup used to be considered a poor man's dish, as sauerkraut, its basic ingredient, is very cheap in Poland.

PEA SOUP

Grochówka

1 cup yellow peas, piece of pork on the bone (e.g. shoulder) about 0.7 lb, 1 onion, 2 carrots, 1 parsnip, 1 celeriac, 1 leek, several potatoes, 2 garlic cloves, allspice, 1 bay leaf, salt, black pepper, marjoram (fresh or dried).

This soup tastes best when made with smoked bacon and it owes its thick texture to the soft-boiled peas. In Poland it is frequently associated with the army, since it is the soldiers' standard dish. It has to be added that it tastes unique when served in a mess tin with a large chunk of bread. In some parts of Poland we can come across army field kitchens from which pea soup is sold to the man in the street. It is very nutritious, so it often constitutes a whole, one-course dinner.

1 Put the peas in a sieve and rinse well in a strong stream of running water. Then put them in a large pot, pour in 3 pints of water and leave overnight to soak.

2 On the following day, cook the peas in the same water with the meat, onion, soup vegetables, finely chopped garlic, herbs and spices. If there is too little water add some more.

3 When the meat is tender remove it from the soup; remove the bones, cut the meat into small pieces and put back in the soup.

4 Peel and dice the potatoes, put them in the soup and cook.

5 Blend the peas and the vegetables until smooth and creamy.

6 Pour the soup into bowls and sprinkle with fresh marjoram.

TOMATO SOUP

Pomidorowa

1 lb beef on the bone, portion of soup vegetables, about 1.5 lb tomatoes or 5 tbsp tomato paste, 1 cup tomato juice, 5 fl oz cream, 1 oz butter, salt, black pepper, sugar.

1 Rinse the meat, put it in 6 pints of cold water, add salt, bring to the boil and simmer over a low heat for about one hour.

2 Half-way through the cooking process add the cleaned and rinsed vegetables.

3 Stew the sliced tomatoes with butter and several spoonfuls of water in a covered pan, over a low heat, for about 30 minutes. Sieve them and add to the strained meat and vegetable stock.

4 Cook for a moment and after removing the dish from the cooker pour in the tomato juice and season the soup with salt, sugar, pepper and cream.

Serve with rice or noodles.

This soup and the broth make a special couple, since the broth is frequently seasoned with tomatoes on the following day. The tomatoes can either be fresh or stewed in butter before they are sieved, but tomato paste can also be used if you prefer a tangier taste. It is served with noodles or rice, seasoned with cream.

MUSHROOM SOUP
WITH SQUARE NOODLES

Grzybowa z łazankami

3 oz mixed dried mushrooms, about 0.5 lb square noodles, 2 vegetable stock cubes, 2 onions, 2 tbsp vegetable oil, salt and black pepper.

I n some regions of Poland this soup is a typical Christmas Eve dish. It is best when made with boletus mushrooms, served clear or with cream. It is a must to serve it with square noodles called "łazanki". It is not an everyday dish, but when it is eaten on other occasions than at a festive meal it can be made with broth or with vegetable and meat stock.

1 Put the well rinsed mushrooms in a pot and pour in 4 pints of water.

2 Add one quartered onion and cook over a low heat for about an hour and a half.

3 Drain off the cooked mushrooms and chop them finely.

4 Boil the noodles following the instructions on the package, strain them, sprinkle with a spoonful of oil and stir to prevent sticking.

5 Peel the other onion, chop it finely and fry in one spoonful of oil until tender. Add the chopped mushrooms, stir and fry for a couple of minutes.
Add the fried mushrooms to the stock together with the stock cubes and bring to the boil.

6 Put the noodles into soup bowls, pour in the hot soup and serve.

Red borsch (beetroot soup) with ravioli

Barszcz z uszkami

Over 0.5 lb meat on the bone (beef, veal or chicken), soup vegetables (2 carrots, 1 parsnip, piece of celeriac, 1 small leek), 4 pt water, 1 lb small beetroots, 1 tbsp apple vinegar or 1/2 teaspoonful citric acid, 2 tbsp marjoram, 2 tbsp sugar, several garlic cloves, salt, black pepper, (2/3 cup thick sour cream – only for the white borsh).

1 Wash and scrub the beetroots well using a brush, put them in boiling water, cook (for about 40 minutes), drain off and cool.

2 Peel the cool beetroots and grate with a vegetable grater.

3 Put the rinsed meat in a large pot of water and bring to the boil over a high heat. Then reduce the heat to low, cover and simmer.

4 When the meat is almost tender add the peeled and rinsed vegetables and the cloves of garlic and cook everything until tender.

5 Remove the cooked meat and vegetables from the stock and add the grated beetroots, citric acid (or vinegar), sugar, salt and pepper and cook for several minutes over a low heat.

6 Strain the borsh using a colander and season with marjoram.

This is a clear soup served with ravioli, but it can also be thickened with cream and then served with boiled potatoes (separately cooked), kidney beans or quartered, hard-boiled eggs.

Ravioli: *approx 1 lb flour, 1 egg, 2 oz dried mushrooms, 1/3 onion, 1 tbsp butter, salt, vegetable oil.*

1 Put the well-rinsed mushrooms in a pot, soak them in water for 1-2 hours and cook in the same water until tender.

2 Drain off the cooked mushrooms, let them cool, dice them finely and then fry in butter with chopped onion and spices.

3 Make a dough from the flour, egg, half a glass of lukewarm water and a pinch of salt, knead it well and then roll out thinly.

4 Cut it into squares and arrange a bit of the stuffing on each.
Pinch the edges of the squares to form the ravioli.

5 Boil the ravioli in salted water with a bit of oil until they float to the surface. Take them out with a draining spoon.

*I*n regions where mushroom soup is not a traditional Christmas Eve dish beet-root borsh is made for this festive dinner. It has a special sweet and sour taste. It is also served at wedding receptions, christening parties and other family gatherings. Naturally, it is also eaten on an everyday basis, often served with tiny dumplings, with meat, or with cabbage and mushrooms during Lent. It is an ambition of every good housewife to make the ravioli as tiny as possible. The Polish name for this type of ravioli is "uszka", which means small ears, because their shape resembles animals' ears. Making them is a very time-consuming activity which sometimes takes several hours.

TRIPE SOUP
Flaki

2 lb beef tripe, 1 lb beef (shin), approx 1.5 lb entrecote or oxtail, soup vegetables (0.7 lb): carrot, parsnip, celeriac, 1 tbsp lard, 2 tsp marjoram, 1 tsp hot red pepper, 1/8 tsp ground ginger, pinch of ground nutmeg, salt, black pepper.

1 Clean the tripe well. Rub with salt and rinse several times in running water. Then put in a pot of cold water, bring to the boil and strain. Repeat the procedure again.

2 Put the tripe in boiling water, add salt and cook for 4 hours.

3 When the tripe is tender put it aside to cool in the water in which it was cooked; then strain it and cut into thin strips.

4 Cook beef and vegetable stock.

5 Pour the stock through a strainer, add the cut tripe, the cooked vegetables cut into strips and the finely cut beef without bones. Cook all the ingredients for a while.

6 Melt a spoonful of lard, add hot pepper, fry for a couple of minutes, add to the tripe and bring to the boil. Season the dish with salt, pepper, nutmeg, powdered marjoram and ginger.

*T*his exquisite and tasty dish may give rise to certain controversies. Yet, if we willingly eat eggs, why not try this delicacy? In fact, this is a superb, meaty soup made from ox stomachs, cleaned, cut into strips and cooked in stock with nutmeg and ginger. The recipe for this dish probably stems from poverty, since in the past all animal parts were prepared in such a way that they could be eaten. This soup was known as early as the 15th century, in the times of Queen Jadwiga, and it is still eaten, usually during grand receptions, because it takes a long time to make.

Frequently tripe is served in clear broth. However, some people like it thickened with flour and parmesan cheese and then baked in the oven.

We have an expression in Poland that says something is "boring as tripe with oil". Its origins are unknown, but we can guess that some unskilled or malicious hostess must have treated someone to a badly made dish of tripe.

"KRUPNIK" BARLEY SOUP

Krupnik

4 oz barley grits, 1/2 lb bones, 1.5 oz butter, parsley, 1 tbsp dill, salt, several dried mushrooms, 1/2 lb soup vegetables, 3 pt water, 1/2 lb potatoes.

1 Cook stock from mushrooms soaked in water, bones and vegetables and pour it through a strainer.

2 Cut the cooked vegetables and mushrooms into strips.

3 Rinse the barley, put in cold water and cook until sticky adding half of the butter.

4 Cook peeled and diced potatoes in the stock.

5 Add the barley, mushrooms, vegetables and salt.

6 At the end add the remaining butter, chopped parsley and dill.

Krupnik is a mild, substantial soup with slightly overcooked barley grits that give it its characteristic texture. It is particularly tasty when made with Krakow barley grits that are very fine, but grits of larger granulation will also do. The secret of making a good krupnik consists in adding the proper amount of grits, which absorb water and expand. If we lose the sense of proportion, we may get a thick custard instead of a soup. This soup is often recommended as part of a light diet, as it is a real balm for the stomach.

"ZHUR" SOUR RYE SOUP WITH SAUSAGE AND EGG

Żurek

4 oz wholemeal rye or oat flour, 1/2 lb bacon, sausage or ham, 1/2 lb soup vegetables, 1 garlic clove, salt, 1 oz wheat flour, 1 tbsp cream.

1 Preparation of the sour rye juice: mix the rye flour with approx 1 pint of boiled water, pour into a stoneware pot and put aside in a warm place. The liquid is ready when it has a sour taste and a nice smell.

2 Cook a concentrated stock using vegetables and cold meats and pour it through a strainer.

3 Add 2.5 pints of water and 1-2 cups of sour rye juice.

4 Thicken the "zhur" with wheat flour blended with cream and add salt.

5 At the end put in the meats and garlic pressed with salt.

Serve with ground horseradish and hard-boiled eggs.

17

WHITE BORSCH WITH WHITE SAUSAGE

Biały barszcz

SOUR RYE JUICE: *1/2 lb rye flour, some bread crusts, 2 pt water.*

Make the sour rye juice two days ahead.

1 Mix the flour with warm boiled water.

2 Put some bread crusts on top and keep in a warm place for 48 hours.

WHITE BORSH: *2 cups sour rye juice, 1 garlic clove, 2 tbsp ground horseradish, 3/4 cup cream, 2 tbsp soup seasoning, 5 cups stock (e.g. from boiled ribs), cress to garnish, 1 cup finely diced ham, 25 pieces of white sausage (each about 1 in long), salt, black pepper.*

1 Pour the stock into the sour rye juice, add garlic and horseradish, add soup seasoning and bring to the boil.

2 Add the cream, finely cut ham and pieces of white sausage.

3 At the end season with salt and pepper.

4 Before serving garnish the borsh with cress.

It can be served with hard-boiled eggs.

Each housewife has in her repertoire a soup which is her masterpiece and "trademark". In the same way Poland as a country also has such a soup. It is undoubtedly the "zhur", a soup made with sour rye juice that gives it a characteristic taste and acidity. It is eaten in numerous regions of Poland and white borsh is one variety. The best "zhur" is made with sausage, smoked bacon, ribs, pig tail, as well as with the stock obtained from cooking ham or white sausage. It can be served clear with a side dish of boiled potatoes. It may also be made with vegetable and meat stock. In some households borsh is seasoned with cream or milk, in others with chopped bacon or bacon fried with or without chopped onions. Some sliced sausage, boiled potatoes and hard-boiled eggs can also be added to a bowl of "zhur".

This excellent soup is a Polish dish without which no Easter breakfast would be complete. But of course it is eaten all year round, though sometimes in its more modest variety made with onion stock, with potatoes boiled in the soup and with just a little streaky bacon or pork fat. It is then called "zalewajka". In Polish this word is derived from "zalewać" (to pour), since sour rye juice is poured into the dish.

It also tastes great at 4 in the morning, after a night-long revelry during which a lot of alcohol was consumed, since it restores your strength and is a good hangover cure.

COLD HERRING SOUP
WITH HOT POTATOES

Zupa śledziowa

1 onion, 1 large bay leaf, 3 grains of allspice, 1/3 tsp black peppercorns, 3 tbsp sugar, 1/3 tsp white mustard seeds, 2 cups water, 3 tbsp vinegar, 1.6 lb mildly salted herring fillets, 1 lb potatoes, 1 pt cream.

1 Pour cold water over the herring fillets and leave them to soak for at least 2 hours in the refrigerator. If the herrings are very salty, they should soak much longer, even for 24 hours.

2 In the meantime prepare the marinade. Pour cold water into a pot with a lid, add thinly sliced onion, a bay leaf, allspice, black peppercorns, sugar, vinegar and mustard seeds.

3 Cook the marinade for 10 minutes over a low heat and then leave to cool.

4 To the cold marinade add cold cream and the soaked herrings cut into inch-long strips.

5 Leave the soup in the refrigerator for several hours.

6 Before serving boil potatoes in their jackets and then peel them.

Serve the cold herring soup with hot potatoes.

CHICKEN POLISH STYLE

Kurczak po polsku

1 whole chicken, 1.1 lb dry bread rolls, 1/2 glass milk, chicken liver, egg, 2 tbsp chopped dill, 1.1 lb butter or margarine, salt.

1 Rinse the chicken well, dry it and sprinkle with salt inside and out.

2 Soak the bread in milk, squeeze and then mince together with the liver.

3 To the minced paste add an egg yolk, a teaspoonful of butter, dill, salt and blend well.

4 Whisk the egg white to a foam, add to the blended paste and mix well.

5 Stuff the chicken with the filling and sew up the opening or tie crosswise with a thin string scalded in boiling water.

6 Place the chicken in a baking dish, cover with slices of butter and put in a preheated oven.

7 Roast until golden brown, from time to time basting with the melted fat and some water.

You can arrange peeled potatoes around the chicken. They will bake simultaneously. A perfect side dish for the chicken is, for instance, a cucumber salad with sour cream.

Poultry is very popular in Poland because it is affordable and the preparation does not take long. It is eaten on daily basis and on special occasions. The dish called "chicken Polish style" is baked in the oven. It is stuffed with poultry livers mixed with bread. It is not eaten too often though. The most popular poultry dishes include roast chicken or fired chicken-breast fillets.

DUCK WITH APPLES
Kaczka z jabłkami

1 duck (4-4.5 lb), 1.5 lb cooking apples, salt, freshly ground black pepper, marjoram, 3 tbsp lard, 1 sprig rosemary.

1 Rinse and dry the duck, rub it inside and out with salt, pepper and rosemary.

2 Cover it and put aside in a cool place for 1-2 hours.

3 Heat the lard in a deep pan and sear the duck on all sides.

4 Cut the peeled apples into quarters, remove the cores and dredge in marjoram.

5 Fill the seared duck with apples and sew up or clip the opening well.

6 Place the duck in a roasting dish and roast for about two hours at 220°C, baste it occasionally with the gravy from the bottom of the dish.

7 15 minutes before the end of the roasting time arrange pieces of apple and orange around the duck.

DUCK WITH RED CABBAGE

Kaczka z czerwoną kapustą

1 duck, 4 tbsp lard, 1 small red cabbage, 2 oz pork fat, 2 onions, 1 tbsp flour, 1 tbsp margarine, 1 cup red wine, salt, sugar, black pepper, lemon juice, 15 grapes.

*T*his is a traditional old Polish dish and although it is heavy on the stomach it is a real delicacy when well made. Stewed duck with apples used to be served mostly in the manor-houses of the gentry. The dish was a side dish accompanying the main course which usually consisted of a wild boar or a pig also stuffed with apples.

1 Remove the wings, neck and vertebral column of the duck.

2 Rinse and dry the halves of the duck, salt and fry in lard.

3 Chop the giblets and one onion, fry in margarine until golden, add water and cook for 30 minutes.

4 Place the fried duck halves in a saucepan, add the giblet stock and stew until the meat is almost tender.

5 Shred the cabbage and scald with boiling water, season with salt and sprinkle with lemon juice.

6 Cut the pork fat finely, fry with chopped onion and sprinkle with flour.

7 Add the fried pork fat with onion and the cooked giblets to the cabbage, pour in the wine and stew over low heat. Season with salt, pepper and sugar.

8 Put the cabbage on the duck and stew the dish for 40 more minutes.

9 At the end of the process add the grapes.

ROAST BEEF OLD POLISH STYLE

Staropolska pieczeń wołowa

9-10 lb beef for roasting, 1 piece of pork fat, several carrots, several parsnips, several onions, 2.6 pt vinegar, salt, saltpetre, coriander, juniper berries, black peppercorns, allspice, bay leaves, cloves.

1 Pound the meat well, rub with salt and saltpetre, place in a bowl and put aside in a moderately cool place for two days. During this time the meat should be turned over every couple of hours.

2 Boil the vinegar with a teaspoonful of saltpetre, some coriander, juniper berries, pepper, allspice, cloves and a bay leaf. When the marinade cools a bit pour it over the meat, cover it and put an extra weight on the lid.

3 Place the beef for a week in a cold place and turn the meat over every day to let it marinate evenly.

4 Line the bottom and sides of an oven-pan with slices of streaky bacon or pork fat and put the meat into it. Add chopped carrots, parsnips and onions.

5 Put the pan in a preheated oven and roast the meat until tender and golden-brown on all sides. From time to time baste with the marinade.

The roast is also tasty, and perhaps even tastier, if before roasting the beef is larded with thickly cut smoked pork fat.

The secret of good roast beef is connected with the kind of meat. If it is mature and well seasoned it may really melt in your mouth. Polish housewives know that secret. To make sure that the beef is tender it should be put aside for a quarter of an hour or so after it is roasted.

"Zrazy" beef rolls
old Polish style
Staropolskie zrazy wołowe

3.3 lb beef for rolls, 5 oz fresh pork fat or smoked bacon, 7 oz pickled gher-kins, 3.5 oz onion, 2-3 dried mushrooms, 4 tbsp vegetable oil, 2 tbsp flour, 3/4 cup cream, 2 tbsp mixed spice, salt, black pepper.

Beef "Zrazy", most fre-quently rolled, are an icon of Polish cuisine. Usually they are served with grits and gherkins and in this form they are known in Europe as "Polish" meat rolls. In Poland they became popular in the 18th century.

1 Cut the meat against the grain into 10 slices of even thickness and pound each slice with a mallet carefully to avoid perforating the meat.

2 On each piece of meat place a thin slice of fat or bacon and a strip of gherkin, then roll the meat tightly.

3 Skewer the meat rolls with metal skewers or tie with white thread and dredge with spices and flour.

4 Fry in oil until golden and then arrange the rolls tightly in a flat saucepan.

5 Pour in some boiling water to reach the level of 2/3 of the meat layer and add the mushrooms soaked in water.

6 Add the chopped, fried onions and stew the meat until tender.

7 When the rolls are tender remove them and the mushrooms from the saucepan. Remove the thread or the skewers from the rolls, chop the mushrooms finely and add to the sauce.

8 Thicken the sauce with cream blended with flour, bring to the boil and season.

9 Heat up the meat rolls in the sauce before serving.

The dish can, for instance, be served with fluffy grits and a green salad.

PORK CHOPS

Kotlety schabowe

4 pork chops (on or off the bone as preferred), 1 egg, 1 tbsp flour, 5-6 tbsp breadcrumbs, fat for frying, salt, black pepper.

1 Pound the rinsed and dried chops with a mallet and season them with salt and pepper.

2 Coat each chop in flour, dip in egg stirred with a fork, then dredge in breadcrumbs.

3 Immediately place the coated chops in a frying-pan with hot fat and fry on both sides until golden brown.

4 Serve the chops at once with potatoes and stewed cabbage.

5 The fried chops can also be transferred to a saucepan with a little bit of fat, then sprinkled with water and kept covered over a medium heat for about 15 minutes.

This is not a typically Polish dish, but is so popular that many Poles think it is. A pork chop with potatoes and stewed cabbage is a dinner dish whose popularity is conditioned by several factors. Firstly, it is tasty and easy to make. Secondly, it takes little time to make. Thirdly, almost anyone can make it. Still, experienced housewives know that the "ordinary" pork chop is good only when it is not too thin and not too thick, when the coating sticks well to the meat and when it is fried in really hot fat, preferably lard. As far as the cabbage is concerned, everyone prepares it according to their own taste.

PORK "MACZANKA" CRACOVIAN STYLE

Maczanka krakowska

1 lb pork chop, lard or clarified butter for frying, 1 tbsp flour, 3-4 onions, 8 slices of white bread cut at an angle, salt, black pepper, caraway seeds, ketchup.

1 Wash the meat and remove the bones.

2 Rub it with salt, pepper and caraway, wrap it in foil and put in the fridge for 24 hours.

3 Then dredge it in flour and fry in lard or butter adding also the previously removed bones to improve the taste.

4 Pour in several tablespoons of water, cover and stew until tender; then remove the meat from the sauce and cut it into slices.

5 Cut the remaining meat from the bones, chop finely, add to the meat sauce, heat up and season.

6 Put the slices of white bread in the sauce for a couple of minutes to soak well.

7 Peel the onions, slice and then cut the slices into halves; fry in lard or butter until golden.

8 On a platter arrange alternate slices of meat, slices of bread and onion rings.

9 Top the dish with the sauce. It can be served with ketchup.

Maczanka is a typically Cracovian dish, which is reflected in its name, and it offers an interesting idea for serving pork roast. Its taste depends on the preparation of the meat, which is roasted in the oven. The best meat for this is pork neck or loin prepared with a large amount of sauce. Each diner is served a halved bread-roll with a slice of meat placed inside and topped with sauce.

LIVER AND ONIONS

Wątróbka z cebulką

Pork liver, 2 onions, half an apple, flour, salt, black pepper, oil for frying.

1 Peel the onions and the apple, cut into half-slices and sear in hot fat.

2 Cut the rinsed and dried liver into portions, dredge in flour and fry with the onions and apple.

3 Add some water and stew for some time.

4 When the liver is tender season with salt and pepper (N.B. Raw liver should not be salted as it will become tough when fried!).

Serve the liver with potatoes and a salad of your choice. It can also be eaten with bread, either hot or cold.

*O*ffal *is commonly eaten in Poland and liver is by far the most popular type. It is tasty and it can be prepared according to the personal preferences of the diners – rare, medium-rare or well-done. At the end of the frying process onions are added and the two flavours blend with one another. When you order liver in a restaurant do not be surprised that it is not seasoned, since in order to prevent it from becoming tough salt has to be added after cooking.*

BOILED PORK KNUCKLE

Golonka gotowana

4 medium-sized pork knuckles, 2 carrots, 2 parsnips, 1 small celeriac, 2 onions, 2-3 bay leaves, 5 allspice grains, 5 black peppercorns, salt.

1 Clean and wash the knuckles well.

2 Place them in a pot, pour in salted boiling water, cover and cook over a low heat, allowing 20 minutes for each pound of meat.

3 Add the peeled, rinsed and cut vegetables, bay leaves, allspice and pepper, season with salt and cook for a further 20 minutes.

4 Remove the knuckles and serve them with pureed peas, horseradish or with stewed sauerkraut.

This is the favourite dish of beer drinkers. It is very fatty and it is served with horseradish and mustard. Its interesting taste comes from long simmering as a result of which a very tasty and characteristic aspic is formed. In spite of the large amount of fat the meat is very tasty, juicy and tender.

29

ROAST BACON

Pieczony boczek

2 lb uncooked bacon, several garlic cloves, caraway seeds, marjoram, 1 bay leaf, 4-5 allspice grains, salt.

1 Rub the bacon on all sides with garlic ground with salt and place in a oven-pan.

2 Sprinkle with caraway, marjoram, crumbled bay leaf and allspice ground in a mortar. Keep the seasoned meat overnight in the fridge.

3 On the next day cover the bacon with onion slices, add a little bit of water and roast in the oven until the meat is nicely browned.

MEAT RISSOLES

Kotlety mielone

1 lb minced meat (pork and beef), 1 white bread-roll (preferably dry), several tbsp milk, 1 onion, 1 tbsp chopped parsley, 1 egg, breadcrumbs, frying oil, marjoram, salt, black pepper.

*R*issoles made from minced pork and beef with onion and egg constitute yet another home-made dish. In Polish households they enjoy great popularity and are treated as an everyday dish. They are not usually served at parties. Maybe because of their "common" nature they are not so easily found on restaurant menus. They can be found though and they are certainly worth trying.

1 Place the bread-roll in a bowl, pour in some milk and put the bowl aside letting the bread soak well.

2 Put the meat into a large bowl and stir well with a fork to crush the lumps.

3 Add the squeezed bread-roll and a raw egg to the meat and stir well.

4 Add the chopped parsley and spices, stir well and check if the meat is well salted and if it has a distinct taste.

5 Peel the onion, chop it finely and fry in oil until tender; then stir it into the meat mixture.

6 Form meat rissoles, dredge them in breadcrumbs and fry in hot oil on both sides.

Traditional "Bigos" Cabbage Stew

Bigos staropolski

4 lb white cabbage, 4 lb sauerkraut, 2 lb red meat (fifty-fifty pork and beef, possibly some venison), 2 lb sausage (ordinary, hunter's style or Silesian style), 1 lb smoked bacon, several wild mushrooms (fresh or dried), black peppercorns, salt, bay leaves, 1/2 lb onion.

1 Put the sauerkraut and the shredded fresh cabbage in a large pot. Add pepper, salt, mushrooms soaked in water and bay leaves (possibly add some water) and stew everything for a very long time until tender (2-3 hours).

2 Melt the chopped bacon slightly in a frying-pan and add the chopped onions, diced meat and sausage.

3 Add the seared meat, bacon and sausage to the cabbage along with the fat from the frying-pan and stew as long as possible (the longer the better) – the best way is to do it with breaks over several days. While stewing the "bigos" one can pour in some dry red wine from time to time.

The ready dish is thick and dark brown. When served on a plate, no juice should be visible.

If you ask 10 Polish people about a typically Polish dish, 9 of them are bound to say "bigos". It has been known in Poland for centuries. Some say that it was brought to this country from Lithuania by King Ladislas Jagiello, others claim that it came to us with Queen Bona. It was eaten in the manor houses of the nobility, at the royal courts and in burgers' and peasants' households.

The taste of the "bigos" stew largely depends on the amount, quality and diversity of meat and cold cuts added to it. In old Polish cuisine it was customary to add to the stew the leftovers of exquisite roasts and cold cuts which greatly improved the taste of the dish. In the past "bigos" would always be made without a roux and without tomato paste which was unknown in those times.

Some people season "bigos" with caraway seeds, marjoram, allspice, prunes, red wine and tomato paste. It is also customary to add some plum jam. According to some recipes the weight of the added meat should be equal to that of the cabbage. "Bigos" can be made of sauerkraut only, but then it is often too sour. To prevent this the sauerkraut should be rinsed in running water or even first boiled in water.

"Bigos" is one of very few dishes that do not lose their taste quality when reheated many times. On the contrary, each time it is reheated the consistency improves. In old Polish cuisine, particularly during hunting parties, the so-called "bigos with a cheer" was known. It was a custom that consisted in reheating the previously prepared dish in a pot whose lid was thoroughly smeared with a dough. A loud "shot" of the lid caused by the growing pressure inside the pot meant that the dish was ready to eat. Traditionally, "bigos" is eaten with bread.

"GOŁĄBKI" STUFFED CABBAGE ROLLS

Gołąbki

1 white or Savoy cabbage with loose leaves, onions, 0.6 lb minced pork, 1 egg, 3/4 cup rice, 2 tbsp butter, 0.4 lb uncooked bacon, 2 cups meat or vegetable stock, 0.6 lb tomatoes or some tomato paste, allspice, bay leaves, 2 garlic cloves, Salt, black pepper.

1 Put the cabbage in a pot of boiling water; while boiling successively remove the surface leaves as they soften. Cut off the protruding parts of the thick midribs.

2 Cook the rice for 10 minutes in a large amount of water, then strain and cool it.

3 Peel the onions, chop them and fry lightly in half of the butter.

4 Add the onions and a raw egg to the meat, season with pepper and blend very well with the rice.

5 Place portions of the stuffing on the cabbage leaves, fold the two opposite edges of the leaves and roll them.

6 Line the bottom of a saucepan with bacon slices and with the torn or less shapely cabbage leaves and arrange the cabbage rolls tightly.

7 Pour meat or vegetable stock into the saucepan, add several allspice grains and bay leaves, cover and stew over a low heat.

8 Wash and slice the tomatoes; half-way through the stewing process sieve them into the dish with the cabbage rolls.

9 At the end season the sauce with pressed garlic.

The Polish name of the dish, "gołąbki", means pigeons. Yet the dish has nothing in common with these birds which dwell in Krakow in large numbers. The dish is interesting, but its preparation is rather time-consuming. The cooked cabbage leaves with stuffing made from rice and meat are served with tomato or mushroom sauce. Sometimes the rice is replaced with grits. This is perhaps the most Polish of home-made dishes. It evokes associations with a warm, cosy kitchen and a grandma serving a steaming plate of food to her guests.

HOME-MADE LARD

Smalec domowy

1 lb pork fat, 1/2 lb smoked bacon, 1 ring of country sausage, 2 small onions, 3-4 garlic cloves, 1 cooking apple.

The lard is made from diced pork fat, bacon, onions and other ingredients chosen according to taste. In some regions these include apples, prunes, herbs or minced meat or sausage. Some restaurants serve bread and vessels of home-made lard before the meal arrives. Unfortunately, it is a very high-calorie dish and therefore filling. This should be kept in mind when you eat it before the main course.

1 Dice the pork fat, bacon and sausage finely.

2 Put the fat into a saucepan or deep frying-pan and melt it over low heat stirring all the time.

3 When the skin is floating in fat add bacon and sausage and the quartered garlic cloves and onions.

4 Cook the ingredients over low heat until golden-brown.

5 Turn off the heat and remove the stewed pieces of garlic and onions.

6 Grate the peeled apple finely and stir it into the liquid lard.

7 Pour the contents of the saucepan very carefully into a jar or stoneware bowl. When it cools down put it into the fridge to let the lard set.

The lard should be salted according to taste, and of course served on a large slice of bread.

SAUERKRAUT WITH PEAS

Kapusta z grochem

1.5 lb sauerkraut, 3/4 cup shelled peas, 1 onion, 6 tbsp oil for frying, salt, black pepper.

1 Pour boiling water over the peas and cook over low heat until tender. The peas can then be sieved or left whole.

2 Chop the sauerkraut, pour 2 cups of water over it and cook over low heat until tender.

3 Mix the hot sauerkraut with the peas.

4 Peel and chop the onion, fry it lightly in oil and add to the sauerkraut.

5 Season the dish with salt and pepper, stir and bring to the boil again.

6 When the dish is ready leave it in a cool place until the next day.

Note: the best way of processing the peas before cooking is to rinse them and leave overnight in water to soak.

*I*n Poland the colloquial expression "peas and cabbage" denotes a mixture of different unmatched elements and is a synonym of mess and chaos. In spite of this, the dish is delicious and its nature does not reflect the above-quoted idiom in the least . It can be served with melted pork fat, bacon or fried, diced onions or without such seasoning during Lent. In some regions of Poland it is also a typical Christmas Eve dish.

SAUERKRAUT WITH MUSHROOMS

Kapusta z grzybami

2 lb mild sauerkraut, 3 oz dried mushrooms, 2 onions, 3 tbsp butter or vegetable oil, 1 tbsp flour, salt, black pepper.

This Christmas Eve dish is also frequently eaten in early autumn when Polish forests abound with mushrooms. Of course, it tastes best with boletus mushrooms, but its enthusiasts also make it with birch boletus and bay boletus mushrooms.

1 Squeeze the sauerkraut lightly (leave the juice for seasoning), chop and cook until tender with two cups of water.

2 Rinse the mushrooms, pour hot water on them and put aside for 2 hours; then cook until tender.

3 Cut the cooked mushrooms into strips and add to the sauerkraut together with the mushroom stock.

4 Peel, chop and fry the onions in butter until golden, then sprinkle with flour and stir.

5 Add this roux to the sauerkraut and bring to the boil. At the end season with salt, pepper and, if necessary, with sauerkraut juice.

CABBAGE AND MUSHROOM PANCAKES

Krokiety z kapustą i grzybami

BATTER: *2 eggs, 1 cup milk, 1 cup water, 1.5 cup flour, 1 tbsp oil for frying (optional; it prevents the pancakes from sticking to the pan), pinch of salt.*

1 Blend all the ingredients well (preferably in a food processor). If you separate the egg yolks and whites and whisk the whites to a foam, which is added to the batter just before frying, the pancakes will be fluffier.

2 Grease the frying-pan lightly, heat well and turn down the heat.

3 Fry the pancakes, one at a time, pouring in a thin layer of batter. When one side sets toss it and fry on the other side.

FILLING: *2 lb white cabbage, 1/2 lb dried mushrooms, 2 tbsp vegetable oil, 1 onion, salt, black pepper, 1 egg, breadcrumbs.*

1 Shred the cabbage finely, pour cold water over it, add the mushrooms and salt and cook for about half an hour.

2 Strain the cooked cabbage.

3 Dice the peeled onion, fry until golden, add to the cabbage and mushrooms; season the dish with salt and pepper and stir well.

4 Place the filling on the pancakes, fold the sides and roll up.

5 Coat the pancakes in egg and breadcrumbs, then fry until golden in hot oil (about 3 minutes on each side).

Serve hot.

PASTA PARCELS RUSSIAN STYLE

Ruskie pierogi

Dough: *1 lb flour, 2 egg yolks, 3/4 cup lukewarm water.*

Filling: *1.5 lb potatoes, 0.5 lb curd cheese, 2 onions, 1 garlic clove, 2 tbsp butter, 1 tbsp vegetable oil, salt, black pepper.*

1 Cook the peeled potatoes in salted water and then mince them.

2 Mince the curd cheese.

3 Chop the peeled onions and fry in butter together with pressed garlic until tender.

4 Mix the ingredients and stir well, adding quite a lot of salt and pepper.

5 Make a dough from flour, egg yolks, water and a pinch of salt and knead it for about 5 minutes.

6 Roll out thinly and cut into rounds with a large glass.

7 Place a teaspoonful of the filling mixture on each round, pinch the edges together well to form small parcels.

8 Boil them in a large amount of salted water with a drop of oil until they float to the surface.

Serve topped with chopped, fried onions.

SAUERKRAUT AND MUSHROOM PASTA PARCELS

Pierogi z kapustą i grzybami

Dough: *1 lb flour, 1 tbsp oil, 1 egg yolk, warm water (as much as the flour can absorb).*

filling: *3 tbsp (or more) of boiled and ground dried mushrooms, 1 lb sauerkraut, onions, 3 tbsp vegetable oil, 1 egg, salt, black pepper to taste.*

Before serving top the "pierogi" with melted butter.

1 Cook the sauerkraut, chop on a board and fry with chopped onions in hot oil.

2 Add minced mushrooms, pepper, salt and an egg; stir well and let it cool.

3 Place the stuffing on thin rounds cut out with a glass in the rolled-out dough and pinch the edges of the "pierogi" together.

4 Boil them in salted water.

FRUIT PASTA PARCELS

Pierogi z owocami

6 cups wheat flour, 1 egg yolk, pinch of salt, sugar, warm, boiled water, blueberries or strawberries.

1 Sift the flour onto a kneading board.

2 Add an egg yolk, a pinch of salt and some water in order not to make the dough too stiff.

3 Knead and roll out.

4 Cut into rounds using a glass or pastry cutter.

5 In the center of each round arrange some fruit and sprinkle it with sugar.

6 Fold the rounds and pinch the edges together well.

7 Arrange the "pierogi" on a lightly floured board and cover with a cloth to prevent them from drying.

8 Toss the "pierogi" in batches into salted boiling water, stir and cook for about 5 minutes after they float to the surface.

9 Take the "pierogi" out with a draining spoon.

Serve topped with cream or yoghurt.

These pasta parcels known as "pierogi" are very popular in Poland. They can be made with meat, cabbage, mushrooms, cheese, potatoes, buckwheat, spinach, fruit or just anything that a housewife decides to fill them with. The most popular ones, however, are the Russian style pierogi, which our Eastern neighbours call Polish

style "pierogi". They are made with potatoes, curd cheese and fried onions. Yet the homeland of pierogi is not Poland but China. The idea of stuffing pieces of pasta dough with different fillings travelled from China through Russia, Poland and farther, to Western Europe. The name "pierogi" is derived from the old Slavonic word "pir" meaning a feat or a ritual dough, since in the past pierogi were made for various festivals. Each festival had its special pierogi of different shape and with a different filling. There were the so-called "kurniki" (hen cots) made for weddings. They were large and contained various different fillings, but always including chicken. "Knysze", on the other hand, were connected with mourning and were served during funeral receptions. "Kolatki" were baked in January to celebrate the New Year and the old pagan festival of Kolady. Finally, there were also regional varieties of pierogi in different parts of Poland, such as "hreczuszki", "sanieszki" and "socznie". Every year, in mid-August, a two-day pierogi festival is held in the Small Market Square in Krakow. Consumers and an appointed jury assess the pierogi and choose the best ones. The choice is not an easy one, since the exhibitors surprise the public with a plethora of tastes. The festival involves a special service in St. Mary's for Cracovian restaurant owners.

RICE PUDDING WITH APPLES

Ryż z jabłkami

1 cup rice, 3 cups milk, 1 lb cooking apples, lemon juice, 2 oz raisins, cinnamon, salt, sugar, yoghurt or cream.

1 Rinse the rice, put it in hot boiling milk, add a pinch of salt, half a teaspoonful of sugar cover and cook for about 25 minutes.

2 Sprinkle the peeled and grated apples with lemon juice, season with sugar and cinnamon and mix with raisins.

3 Mix the rice with the apple mixture.

Before serving top the dish with cream or yoghurt and sprinkle with sugar and cinnamon.

POTATO DUMPLINGS SILESIAN STYLE

Kluski śląskie

2 lb boiled potatoes, potato flour, 1 egg, salt, 1 tbsp vegetable oil.

1 Mince the boiled potatoes and place them in a large bowl.

2 "Divide" the bowl into quarters. Three quarters should be occupied by the dough and the fourth one with potato flour.

3 Add an egg, a tablespoon of oil and salt and make a smooth dough.

4 Take small chunks of dough and form into balls; in the centre of each make a small hole with your finger.

5 Toss the balls in batches into boiling, salted water, stir and bring to the boil.

6 When the dumplings float to the surface allow them to cook until tender and take them out with a draining spoon.

Serve topped with a mushroom sauce, chopped onions fried in butter or grated cheese.

These gnocchi-like dumplings are made from boiled potatoes like the "kopytka" dumplings, but potato flour replaces here the wheat flour and gives them a distinct texture and taste. Their name is associated with Silesia, because they come from that region, where they are served with roast meat and gravy.

43

"KOPYTKA" GNOCCHI

Kopytka

2 lb potatoes, 1.5 cup flour, 2 eggs, salt.

1 Put the peeled and rinsed potatoes in salted boiling water, cook, strain, evaporate well and mince.

2 Place the minced potatoes on a well-floured kneading board, add flour and eggs and knead well.

3 Roll out the dough into medium thick rolls, flatten them slightly and cut diagonally into diamond-shaped "kopytka".

4 Toss the "kopytka" into boiling salted water, stir to prevent sticking to the bottom and cook for 3 minutes after they float to the surface.

5 When cooked take them out with a draining spoon.

Serve topped with butter or lard or your favourite kind of sauce and with a side dish of salad.

These boiled potato gnocchi have a characteristic shape resembling the hoof of a roe-deer, hence their Polish name "kopytka". This apparently simple recipe may nevertheless cause some problems to those who do not have much experience with cooking. If too much flour is used they will be rock hard and if too little is used they will turn to a pulp. The secret is also connected with the timing. Once the dough is made, "kopytka" should be cooked immediately.

44

POTATO PANCAKES

Placki ziemniaczane

2 lb potatoes, 1 medium onion, 2 egg yolks, 2 tbsp wheat flour, salt, black pepper, 1/2 cup oil for frying.

*D*epending on the customs and likings in a given household potato pancakes are made in different ways. They can be served with salt, with cream or without, or sprinkled with sugar instead. The pancakes are rather small – the size of a human palm. Sometimes, however, one large pancake, the size of the frying-pan, is made and it is served with goulash and hot spices. It is then called a "Hungarian style pancake".

1 Rinse and peel the potatoes, grate them finely and squeeze gently.

2 Peel the onion and grate as well.

3 Add the onion, flour and egg yolks to the potatoes. Season with salt and pepper and stir well.

4 Form thin pancakes with a spoon in a pan of hot oil and fry on both sides until golden.

Serve with cream, kefir or sprinkled with sugar.

NEW POTATOES WITH SOUR MILK

Młode ziemniaki z kwaśnym mlekiem

2 lb new potatoes, bunch of dill, butter, sour milk.

1 Peel the potatoes or just wash them well and scrub with a brush, as their delicate skin peels off easily.

2 Boil the potatoes in salted water and drain when cooked.

3 Put butter and chopped dill into the pot with potatoes, cover and shake well several times to mix the ingredients thoroughly.

4 Keep the pot for a couple of minutes over a low heat.

Serve with cold sour milk or kefir.
If liked, the boiled potatoes can be sprinkled with chopped chives.
Some people serve the potatoes with a fried egg and top them with bacon rind and fried onions.

On hot summer days it is difficult to imagine a better dish than new potatoes with sour milk. Such potatoes should not be thickly peeled but rather scrubbed. Some people just scrub them with a brush until clean. Then the potatoes retain a special, delicate taste. The addition of dill is a must and they have to be served with a side dish of sour milk.

"BABKA" POTATO CAKE

Babka ziemniaczana

3 lb potatoes, 0.6 lb onions, 1/2 lb white mushrooms, 3 eggs, 4 tbsp vegetable oil, breadcrumbs, marjoram, mixed spices, salt, black pepper.

1 Rinse the peeled potatoes and grate one half of them finely and the other half coarsely.

2 Put the grated potatoes into a large bowl and stir well.

3 Chop the peeled onion and sweat in oil together with finely sliced mushrooms.

4 Add the eggs and 3 heaped tablespoons of breadcrumbs to the potatoes and stir well.

5 At the end blend the stewed onions and mushrooms with the potatoes, add a tablespoon of marjoram, salt, pepper and other spices if liked.

6 Grease a large tin, sprinkle thickly with breadcrumbs and fill with the potato mixture.

7 Bake in the oven for 75 minutes at about 150°C.

8 Place the baked "babka" on a plate; serve hot with a mushroom or tomato sauce and with a salad of your choice.

"PYZY" POTATO DUMPLINGS WITH MEAT
Pyzy ziemniaczane z mięsem

3 lb raw potatoes, 1.5 lb boiled potatoes, 1 lb minced meat, 1 large onion, salt, black pepper, piece of pork fat or bacon to season.

This is yet another dish made with potatoes – this time combining the boiled ones and the raw, grated ones. The gnocchi have a characteristic greyish colour coming from the raw potatoes. They can be ball-shaped or oblong. The latter, just because of their shape, are called "Zeppelins". They are filled with a stuffing of minced meat.

1 Peel the raw potatoes, grate them and squeeze. Put the potato juice aside until starch sets on the bottom. Then add the starch to the potato paste.

2 Mince the boiled potatoes, mix them with the grated ones, add salt and stir well.

3 Chop the peeled onion finely, fry in oil and add to the minced meat.

4 Season the stuffing, then sear it and leave to cool.

5 Use the potato dough to form small clumps, place some stuffing on each, stick the edges together and roll into balls.

6 Cook the "pyzy" in boiling salted water for 10-15 minutes.

Serve topped with melted pork fat or bacon.

STEAMED YEAST DUMPLINGS   *Kluchy na lumpie*

1 lb flour, 1 cup milk, approx 1 oz yeast, 2.5 tbsp margarine, 2 eggs, 1/2 tsp sugar, salt to taste.

1 Grind the yeast well with a table-spoon of milk and a tablespoon of flour and put aside to rise in a warm place.

2 Mix together the rest of the flour and milk, adding eggs and salt; mix with the raised yeast and knead well.

3 Add the melted margarine; knead the dough again, put aside and let it rise.

4 Put a cloth on top of a pot of boiling water and tie it well around. Arrange chunks of the dough on the cloth and cover the pot with a large bowl.

5 Steam the dumplings for 20 minutes.

Serve topped with a sauce of your choice.
Such dumplings can also be bought ready-made in food-stores. It is then enough to heat them up before serving.

"ŁAZANKI" SQUARE NOODLES WITH SAUERKRAUT

Łazanki z kapustą

1 cup flour, 3 eggs, 2 lb sauerkraut, 2 onions, 3 tbsp butter, 1/2 teaspoonful caraway seeds, black pepper, salt.

1 Chop the sauerkraut finely, cook and strain.

2 Chop the peeled onions finely and fry in butter until golden.

3 Mix the sauerkraut with onion and season with salt and pepper.

4 Cover and stew for about 20 minutes; at the end season with caraway seeds.

5 Make a rather stiff dough from flour, eggs and some water.

6 Roll the dough out thinly, cut into small diamonds or squares and leave to dry.

7 Boil the "łazanki" in salted water, strain and pour melted butter over them.

8 Butter an ovenproof dish and arrange "łazanki" and sauerkraut in alternate layers.

9 Bake the dish in a hot oven for about 15 minutes.

This dish is known all over Poland and in Krakow it enjoys particular popularity. In each household it is prepared in a slightly different way, but its two basic ingredients, the square noodles and cabbage, remain the same. According to individual taste they can be made either with fresh cabbage or with sauerkraut.

CURD CHEESE PANCAKES

Naleśniki z serem

BATTER: *2 eggs, 1 cup milk, 1 cup water, 1.5 cup flour, 1 tbsp oil for frying (optional; it prevents the pancakes from sticking to the pan), pinch of salt.*

1 Blend all the ingredients well (preferably in a food processor). If you separate the egg yolks and egg whites and whisk the whites to a foam which is added to the batter just before frying, the pancakes will be fluffier.

2 Grease the frying pan lightly, heat well and turn down the heat.

3 Fry the pancakes, one at a time, pouring in a thin layer of batter. When it sets toss it and fry on the other side.

> FILLING: *1 lb curd or cream cheese, 2 egg yolks, sugar, several drops of vanilla flavouring.*

1 Whisk the egg yolks with sugar until smooth and fluffy; gradually add small portions of minced curd or cream cheese and the flavourings blending well all the time.

2 Spread the filling evenly on the pancakes, roll them or fold each of them twice (like a handkerchief) and fry in hot fat on both sides until golden.

Serve sprinkled with icing sugar and topped with cream.

This is a children's favourite sweet dish. In Poland sweet pancakes are also filled with jam or with cream cheese creamed with sugar, cream and sometimes with a raw egg yolk. They can be served hot or cold, topped with cream.

APPLE FRITTERS　　　　　　　*Racuchy z jabłkami*

2 cups kefir, 2 cups flour, 2 eggs, 1 tsp baking powder, 2 or 3 apples.

1 Whisk the egg whites to a stiff foam.

2 Pour the flour mixed with baking powder into a bowl, add kefir and egg yolks.

3 Stir everything gently while adding the foam. The batter should have the consistency of thick cream.

4 Slice the peeled apples thinly, put them into the batter and stir.

5 Heat the fat in a pan; drop small portions of the batter and apples into the pan and fry on both sides over a medium heat until golden. Just before serving sprinkle the fritters with icing sugar.

CARP BAKED IN THE OVEN

Karp z brytfanny

Carp (approx 4 lb), 2–3 garlic cloves, 5 tbsp vegetable oil, celery leaves, parsley, black pepper, salt.

1 Cut the cleaned carp crosswise on the back in 4-5 places.

2 Finely chop the garlic, celery leaves and parsley; add pepper, salt and oil.

3 Use this mixture to fill the carp and the incisions on its back.

4 Place the carp in an oven pan and bake for 20-30 minutes in a medium-heated oven.

5 Halfway through the baking process pour hot water over the fish and then baste regularly with the sauce forming on the bottom of the pan.

Most Polish people cannot imagine a Christmas Eve dinner without carp served fried, baked or in aspic. Also many people eat it only once a year. It is still one of the most popular freshwater fish in Poland. It should be bought as fresh as possible, preferably live. After purchasing it is put in the bath in water where it awaits execution.

POLISH STYLE PIKE OR ZANDER

Szczupak lub sandacz po polsku

3 lb pike (or zander), approx 1 lb vegetables (no cabbage), 4 eggs, 2 tbsp butter, 1 bay leaf, 2 allspice grains, 2 black peppercorns, salt, parsley.

1 Rinse the fish, scale and gut it; cut off the head, fins and tail.

2 Rinse the fish again and slice it.

3 Wash and clean the vegetables, cut them into pieces, place in a shallow saucepan, pour in some cold water, add salt and spices.

4 Cover the vegetables and cook over a high heat until tender; add the fish and cook over a low heat for a further 20 minutes.

5 Peel and chop the hard-boiled eggs.

6 Place the fish on a platter, surround it with strained vegetables and sprinkle with chopped eggs and parsley.

7 Top with fresh butter.

*I*n old Polish tradition fish was very popular and it constituted an important element of the cuisine. However, after World War II, in communist times, fish lost its popularity for a very simple reason, namely it was difficult to obtain. In the so-called fish outlets a sad-looking cod could sometimes be bought, but no one who had any choice would eat it. After the political situation changed, fish made a comeback on the Polish table and its popularity has been growing alongside an awareness of healthy lifestyle and diet.

Herrings are a favourite starter at both large and small parties because of their excellent taste and the fact that they go well with Polish vodka. In some Polish households they are also served cold as a main course for dinner. According to a very old tradition, such a main course consists of freshly boiled potatoes served with cold herrings as a side dish. It is a very original combination of tastes.

Herrings with a "coverlet"

Śledzie pod pierzynką

4 tbsp mayonnaise, 4 herring fillets (approx 1 lb), 2 onions, 2 tbsp mustard, 2 tbsp double cream, 2 eggs, 1 tbsp chopped parsley, 2 tbsp vegetable oil.

1 Cut the herring fillets into smaller pieces and arrange them on a platter.

2 Chop the skinned onions finely and after mixing with mustard and oil spread on the fillets.

3 Peel and finely chop the cooled hard-boiled eggs.

4 Mix the mayonnaise with cream and parsley and spread the mixture evenly over the herrings.

5 Sprinkle the dish with chopped eggs.

Herrings with beetroot

Śledzie w buraczkach

1 lb herring fillets, 4 medium onions, 5 beetroots, 5 potatoes, 4 eggs, mayonnaise, lemon juice, olive oil, salt, black pepper.

1 Boil the potatoes and beetroots in their jackets in separate saucepans; grate them coarsely when cool.

2 Hard boil the eggs, let them cool and grate them coarsely.

3 Cut the rinsed herring fillets into squares.

4 Chop the peeled onions.

5 Arrange the cut herrings on the bottom of a bowl, top them with chopped onions and sprinkle with lemon juice and olive oil.

6 Then arrange on top half the grated beetroot, the grated potatoes and then the other half of the beetroot.

7 Season the dish with salt and pepper and garnish lavishly with mayonnaise.

8 Sprinkle the top with grated eggs and put into the fridge.

CHANTERELLE MUSHROOMS WITH CREAM

Kurki w śmietanie

2 lb chanterelle mushrooms, 1 large onion, 1/4 pack butter, 7 fl oz double cream, 2-3 tbsp chopped dill, salt, black pepper.

1 Shake the sand off the mushrooms, rinse them quickly in a sieve and dry with a paper towel.

2 Cut the large caps into several pieces and leave the smaller ones as they are.

3 Chop the peeled onion finely.

4 Heat the butter in a deep frying pan, fry the onion until tender, add the mushrooms and fry, stirring from time to time until the water evaporates from the pan (10-15 minutes).

5 Add the dill, salt and freshly ground pepper, pour in the cream and cook for a couple more minutes. Turn off the heat when a thick sauce is formed.

Serve immediately as a separate dish or as part of the main course with boiled potatoes, fried fillets or roast veal.

SAUERKRAUT AND CARROT SALAD

Sałatka z kiszonej kapusty i marchewki

1 lb sauerkraut, 1/2 lb carrots, 1 tbsp sugar, 1 tbsp soy or sunflower oil, 1 spoonful chopped parsley.

1 Finely grate the peeled and rinsed carrots and mix with the sauerkraut.

2 Add oil and sugar and stir well.

3 Transfer the salad to a bowl and sprinkle with chopped parsley.

This salad is very popular in Poland for various reasons, among which the fact that it is so easy to make. In Polish cuisine meat and fish are frequently combined with sour ingredients. That is why sauerkraut salad occupies an important position on our national menu.

RED CABBAGE SALAD

Sałatka z czerwonej kapusty

1 small red cabbage, salt, sugar, black pepper, 2 apples, 2 tbsp vegetable oil, 1 onion, parsley.

1 Bring salted water to the boil in a saucepan; in the meantime shred the cabbage finely.

2 Toss it into the boiling water and cook for 5 minutes, then strain and leave to cool.

3 Coarsely grate the peeled apples.

4 Cut the peeled onion into halves and slice the halves thinly.

5 Mix all the ingredients together and season.

6 Place the salad in a bowl, sprinkle with oil and chopped parsley.

VEGETABLE SALAD WITH MAYONNAISE

Sałatka jarzynowa

1 can green peas, 1 onion, 2 eggs, 1 medium pickled gherkin, 4 tbsp mayonnaise, salt, pepper, garlic clove.

1 Drain the peas in a sieve.

2 Dice the peeled onion finely.

3 Hard boil the eggs, let them cool, peel and dice them.

4 Dice the cucumber.

5 Put all the ingredients into a bowl and mix with mayonnaise; add salt, pepper and pressed garlic.

This salad is both simple and delicious.

There was a time when this salad was so popular that no one could imagine a party without it. It was called a "vegetable salad" although there are many salads made from vegetables. Yet for the Polish people this name always denotes the same dish. Its basic ingredients are root vegetables and potatoes. Other additions such as onions, apples, canned peas and eggs are optional. It is seasoned with mayonnaise which makes it pretty heavy.

DRIED FRUIT DRINK

Kompot z suszu

2 pt water, 2 cups dried fruit (apples, pears, prunes, apricots), pinch of cinnamon, 3-5 teaspoonfuls sugar, cloves.

1 Wash the dried fruit well, pour boiled water over it and let it soak for several hours.

2 Add sugar, cinnamon and cloves and cook until tender.

3 After turning off the heat keep covered for several minutes.

"FAWORKI" FRIED SWEETMEATS

Faworki

1/2 lb flour, 3 egg yolks, 3-4 tbsp cream, 1 spoonful spirit, 3 oz icing sugar, salt, 1 lb lard for frying, icing sugar for sprinkling.

1 Make a dough from flour, a pinch of salt, egg yolks, cream and spirit.

2 Roll the dough out very thinly on the kneading board sprinkled with flour and cut with a knife into strips (6x1 in.).

3 Make a long incision in the centre of each strip (about 2 in.) and pass one end of the strip through it.

4 Deep-fry the "faworki" on both sides until golden in very hot lard.

5 Arrange the fried sweetmeats on paper napkins to drain off the excess fat.

6 When still hot sprinkle them lavishly with icing sugar.

"BABA" SPONGE-CAKE

Baba biszkoptowa

2 cups egg whites, 2 cups sugar, 2 cups poppy seeds or ground walnuts, 2 cups flour, approx 1/2 lb margarine, breadcrumbs and butter to grease the baking tin.

1 Whisk the egg whites to a stiff foam adding the sugar gradually while whisking.

2 Pour in the flour, poppy seeds or ground walnuts; at the end add the melted margarine and stir well.

3 Grease a baking tin with butter, sprinkle with breadcrumbs, and pour the batter into it.

4 Bake until golden in a medium-hot oven (preferably at 180°C).

CHEESECAKE WITH MERINGUE "DEW" TOPPING

Sernik z rosą

PASTRY: *2 egg yolks, 1 egg, 3 oz sugar, 3 oz margarine, 1 heaped tbsp lard, 0.7 lb self-rising flour, 2 teaspoonfuls baking powder.*

1 Mix all the ingredients together and blend well.

2 Grease a baking tin and line it with the pastry (also on the sides!).

CHEESE FILLING: *4 egg yolks, 2 eggs, 3 oz margarine, 1 cup sugar, 2 lb cream cheese, 1 packet cream custard powder, 1 cup milk, lemon flavouring.*

1 Mince the cream cheese and blend it with sugar.

2 Add egg yolks, whole eggs, melted margarine (lukewarm), custard powder, milk and lemon flavouring and blend well. The cheese mixture should be quite liquid.

3 Pour the mixture into the tin lined with pastry.

4 Bake for about one hour in a hot oven.

TOPPING: *6 egg whites, 1 cup sugar.*

1 Whisk the egg whites with sugar to a foam and put it on the cheesecake 15 minutes before the end of the baking time.

This is one of the favourite Polish cakes. It is always made from high-fat cream cheese, with butter, sugar, eggs, raisins, candied orange peel and vanilla. The addition of potato flour improves its texture. It is frequently finished with chocolate glaze or sprinkled with icing sugar. Cheesecake Cracovian style has a characteristic checked pattern which is made from thin strips of pastry arranged on top of the cake and iced when the cake is baked.

APPLE PIE CASTELLAN STYLE

Szarlotka kasztelańska

SPONGE-CAKE: *5 eggs, 5 tbsp sugar, 3 tbsp wheat flour, 2 tbsp potato flour, 1 teaspoonful baking powder.*

1 Whisk the egg whites to a stiff foam, add sugar and keep whisking.

2 Add the yolks and keep whisking for a couple of minutes.

3 Add the remaining ingredients and stir gently.

4 Pour the batter into a baking-tin and bake for about 30 minutes at 170°C.

5 Cool after baking.

FILLING: *4 lb apples, 2 packets orange jelly powder, 1 pt double cream, 1 tbsp sugar, 1 packet instant cream-fix.*

1 Coarsely grate the peeled apples and roast them in a pan.

2 Add the jelly powder to the hot apples, stir well and while still hot spread on the sponge-cake.

3 When the apple mixture sets spread a layer of cream whipped with sugar and cream-fix over it.

CHOCOLATE GLAZE: *3 oz margarine, 2 tbsp sugar, 2 tbsp cocoa, 1 egg, almond flakes.*

1 Melt the margarine with sugar and cocoa without bringing the mixture to the boil.

2 Whisk the egg white to a stiff foam, add the yolk and stir gently.

3 Add the whisked egg gradually to the cooled fat stirring all the time.

4 Spread the glaze gently on the cream layer.

5 Keep the cake refrigerated.

HOME-MADE POPPY-SEED CAKE

Makowiec

DOUGH: *4 eggs, 4 tbsp cold water, 4 oz sugar, grated lemon peel, pinch of salt, 5 oz flour, grease for the tin.*

1 Whisk egg yolks and water to a foam, adding 2/3 of the sugar.

2 When the mixture becomes whitish add the lemon peel.

3 Whisk the egg whites with a pinch of salt to a stiff foam adding the remaining sugar towards the end.

4 Add alternative portions of whisked egg whites and flour to the yolk mixture and stir gently.

5 Line a flat baking-tin with greaseproof paper, grease and spread the batter evenly.

6 Place the tin in a pre-heated oven and bake at 200°C for about 12 minutes.

7 Place the baked cake bottom-up on a cloth sprinkled with sugar. Wet the greaseproof paper slightly with water and peel off gently. Roll the sponge-cake (together with the cloth) into a roll and leave to cool.

FILLING: *1/2 lb poppy seeds, approx 1 pt milk, 3 oz butter, 1 egg yolk, 4 oz sugar, 1 packet vanilla sugar, 2 fl oz rum, 4 oz ground almonds.*

1 Rinse the poppy seeds, pour boiling milk on them and cook over a low heat for about 30 minutes.

2 Strain the cooked poppy seeds and mince 3 times.

3 Cream the butter with the egg yolk, sugar and vanilla sugar until fluffy and whitish.

4 Mix the creamed butter with the poppy seeds, add ground almonds and stir well. Add rum at the end.

5 Unwrap the rolled cake and remove the cloth.

6 Spread the cooled poppy-seed filling over the cake and form into a roll again.

CHOCOLATE GLAZE: *3 oz icing sugar, 1 oz cocoa, 2 tbsp hot water, 1 tbsp chopped almonds.*

1 Blend the icing sugar, cocoa and hot water.

2 Add chopped almonds and stir.

3 Spread the glaze on the top and sides of the cake.

This cake evokes thoughts of Christmas, since this is the season when dishes with poppy seeds are made in every Polish household. A classic example is a poppy-seed loaf, which is a kind of roll made with yeast cake and poppy-seed filling with raisins, nuts, almonds and other dried fruit.

THE POPE'S CREAM CAKES

Papieskie kremówki

FLAKY PASTRY: *2 cups flour, 1/2 lb margarine, 1.5 oz yeast, 4 tbsp cream (18% fat).*

1 Spread the flour on a kneading board, add the margarine and chop.

2 Add the cream and yeast. Knead the pastry and divide it into two parts.

3 Roll out two large squares of pastry and bake in flat baking tins.

CREAM FILLING: *1.6 pt milk, 3 oz butter, 1 cup sugar, 1 large packet of vanilla sugar, 3 heaped tbsp potato flour, 3 heaped tbsp wheat flour, 3 egg yolks.*

1 Take some cold milk and blend with flour and egg yolks.

2 Mix in the remaining ingredients and bring to the boil.

3 Let it cool and spread over one of the baked cakes then cover with the other one. Sprinkle the cake with icing sugar.

The Pope's cream cakes, also known as "Wadowice cream cakes", are delicious cakes with a fluffy vanilla cream. They have made a tremendous career. For Polish people they are a symbol of John Paul II's. He moved all his compatriots during his visit to his hometown of Wadowice when he said, "There was a patisserie there. After our school-leaving exams we used to go and have cream cakes there". Since that time these cakes have become extremely popular both in Poland and abroad and for commercial reasons almost each producer of cakes of this type aspires to call them this name.

SELF-SERVICE RESTAURANT POLAKOWSKI
ul. Miodowa 39

In Miodowa Street, in the district of Kazimierz, you will find a truly unique restaurant. Its domestic atmosphere is emphasized by the fitting interior design, which features, among other things, racks and shelves full of preserves and fresh vegetables that encourage you to try the excellent dishes. There are special pots where the sourdough of "zhur" and "borsch", from which soups are later made, are left to ferment. The high quality food is served by charming ladies in straw hats. What is more, the wonderful smell of the dishes and the way they look make this place truly exceptional. Here we talk about the restaurant with its creator, Dominik Dybek:

What makes the restaurant such a special place?

Above all, the procedure for preparing the dishes. As we want each dish to taste equally good every day, we give our dishes a special kind of certificate, which means that the dish was separately tasted and approved by 4 members of the kitchen staff. At our place each dish has its own history, the same spices are added to it and its appearance and taste do not change. The approval of several people eliminates the risk of mistakes resulting, for instance, from someone's indisposition. Such a procedure is repeated every morning.

Why is the place called Polakowski?

In 1899, Jakub Polakowski had his business in Lvov. It was not a restaurant, however, but a store selling a range of goods which included meat. In the 1920s, the family emigrated to Argentina where they continue to run their business. I met Polakowski here in Kazimierz in 1997, if I remember correctly. I decided to take up his idea and bring it to life on a large scale by creating a chain of restaurants with an identical menu and style. It is in fact the interior design of the place that constitutes the link with Polakowski's store. This chain of restaurants is now being created. In Krakow there are already two restaurants and there will be more. I would also like the Polakowski restaurants to be present in all large cities in Poland, as well as in European metropolises such as Vienna, Paris or London and in the USA.

A self-service restaurant? You have to admit that the word 'restaurant' brings about associations with waiters, rather.

Yes, but the word 'restaurant', which is similar in all languages, makes the place recognizable also among foreigners. And since the objective is to serve the dishes quickly, without unnecessary waiting, we decided not to have any waiting staff and each client orders and takes his dishes to the table himself.

What are the good things that can be eaten at your restaurant?

Everything is tasty and the choice depends on the guest and his preferences. The menu includes traditional Polish dishes such as bigos, pork chops, cabbage, Polish beetroot, pierogi filled with meat or with cabbage and mushrooms or Russian style, pan-

cakes, cabbage rolls, "zhur", beetroot borsh and many other dishes, which include also one Jewish dish, namely chulent. Depending on the season, we also add to the menu some dishes representing international cuisine to allow our clients to become acquainted with other tastes. We also encourage the customers to taste some dishes before making their final choice. And that tasting is on the house!

All dishes are made on the basis of original recipes, including my own, under consultations with the Polakowski family. We do not want to expand the menu. I myself do not trust restaurants which offer a really wide range of dishes. When there are too many dishes it is difficult to maintain good quality, which is our primary objective.

How can you keep the prices of dishes in the Polakowski restaurant low?

Of course maintaining low prices in just one restaurant results in very low profitability, but when a chain of restaurants exists it grows considerably. We focus on clients' full satisfaction by both offering them good value and catering to their tastes.

Well, now the only thing we can do is to invite everybody to the Polakowski restaurant and wish them a wealth of experiences while savouring Polish dishes.

Restaurants serving exquisite Polish food in Krakow

Pod Gruszką – ul. Szczepańska 1
It is said in Krakow that the city originated here, as at the spot where this 14th-century town house is situated the first peg was placed in the ground when the city borders were traced. The restaurant hall resembles the interior of an old, burgher's house, with its decorations, mirrors and portraits. It is also famous for Fontana's Hall, which was once a bathroom for King John Sobieski's beloved wife, Queen Mary. This is an important listed building.
Here we can eat delicious "pierogi" (filled pasta parcels) – Russian style or with cabbage and boletus mushrooms, beef rolls with mushrooms, pork knuckle, pork chops with cabbage, as well as "zhur" (a kind of rye soup) and "bigos" stew served in bowls made from hollowed-out loaves of bread.

Pod Aniołami – ul. Grodzka 35
You can expect angels to take care of the dishes prepared here, which certainly has a positive influence on their flavour. Here can sample delicious Polish soups, such as chicken, red borsh, zhur and mushroom soup with "łazanki" noodles, as well as excellent pork knuckles and "bigos" stew.

Wierzynek – Rynek Główny 15
This is the most famous restaurant in Krakow and its tradition of treating guests to excellent meals dates back to the 14th century. In 1364, the first historic feast took place here. Jan Długosz, a Polish historian, describes it in his chronicle.
Nowadays, customers are welcomed and guided to the restaurant rooms by hostesses wearing costumes inspired by 14th-century attire. The first floor of the restaurant consists of a suite of four rooms: the Clock Hall, the Tatra Hall, the Column Hall and Wierzynek's Hall. The Knight's Hall is also situated on the same level. The second floor comprises the Grand and Small Pompeian Halls and the Club Room. Altogether these halls can seat 400 people, which makes Wierzynek the largest restaurant in Krakow. The excellent cuisine offered here is a combination of Polish tradition and cosmopolitan culinary trends.

Jarema – pl. Matejki 5
The interior design of the restaurant evokes the atmosphere of old manor-houses in Eastern Poland. Its name refers to the wealthiest magnate of the Republic of Poland, an eminent military leader and scientist commemorated also by Sienkiewicz, a Nobel Prize holder, in his novel "By Fire and Sword". The restaurant offers wonderful noodles, dumplings, real sour milk with potatoes and dill, excellent soups and a plethora of other old-style Polish dishes.

Poezja Smaku (Poetry of Taste) – ul. Jagiellońska 5

At this place we recommend savouring the taste of chicken soup and "bigos" stew. You can also have Cracovian cheesecake and apple pie. At this mysterious and, as the name suggests, poetic address, which is divided into smaller rooms for around a dozen or several dozen people, we can catch a glimpse of Krakow's mysteries

Gospoda u Zdzicha – Rynek Główny 24

The interior of this restaurant hidden in the gate of one of Krakow's town houses is in traditional folk style. The wooden tables, benches, stuffed animals and waitresses in folk costumes contribute to this character. The excellent Polish dishes, and the "pierogi" in particular, are very affordably priced and they taste delicious.

Nostalgia – ul. Karmelicka 10

Apart from great "pierogi" we can also eat very good Polish soups, pork chops, pork knuckles and a number of other Polish dishes here. Some of them are made on the basis of old, simple recipes, other dishes are more like "variations on the theme"... The climate of the place with its beautiful interior is pleasant and genuinely nostalgic, inviting us both to ponder and to daydream.

Pod Baranem – ul. Św. Gertrudy 21

The restaurant specializes in Polish cuisine with just a touch of western European cuisine. Particularly worth recommending is the fish smoked in alder-wood smoke and the so-called Cracovian "maczanka", which was honoured with the Galician Taste Academy Award, as well as many other dishes made to order, such as leg of mutton, roast goose or cutlets Lithuanian style.

Elektor Hotel Restaurant – ul. Szpitalna 28

This is not a large restaurant. It can accommodate just 20 people or so, but it easily allows us to imagine that we are in an old aristocratic residence. Here we can eat old-style Polish dishes based on the unique recipes of the family of the Counts Potocki.

Hawełka – Rynek Główny 34

The restaurant serves old Polish dishes. Its speciality is duck Cracovian style served with boletus mushrooms and Cracovian buckwheat grits of course. It is a must to taste the world-famous speciality, mushroom soup served in a hollowed-out loaf of bread.

Morskie Oko – pl. Szczepański 8

Here specialities from Zakopane can be found in the centre of Krakow. The excellent food, extremely pleasant service and live mountain folk music contribute to the impression that in just one moment we feel as if we have landed in the Tatras.

Komnata – ul. Czapskich 5

In this Renaissance-style interior with candles aflame you can eat breakfast, lunch or dinner here, as the restaurant is open from 6.30 a.m. Its specialities include grilled ribs with honey, King Sas's platter and cream of boletus mushroom soup in a hollowed-out royal bread loaf.

Restaurant on Wawel Hill – Wzgórze Wawelskie 9
A number of celebrities – kings, presidents, senators, deputies, company directors and leading businessmen have been treated to meals here. The menu includes Polish and French dishes. The place can also be proud of its wine cellar which can satisfy the tastes of the most demanding connoisseurs.

Sąsiedzi – ul. Szpitalna 40
Here we can eat mostly Polish meat dishes including beef, pork and poultry, as well as fish, potato pancakes and regular pancakes. The owner of the restaurant emphasizes the fact that he uses only the highest quality ingredients without preservatives. The dishes are made using his own, original recipes.

Kawaleria – ul. Gołębia 4
A good selection of salads, excellent soups, such as mushroom soup and "zhur" (a kind of sour rye soup), salmon "pierogi", fried liver and onions… These are just some items on the menu of this restaurant. Here you can also find the Cracovian style "maczanka" awarded a prize during the Małopolska Region Taste Festival, roast meats, fish and tasty desserts including apple pie.

Bohema Artistic Restaurant – ul. Gołębia 2
Feasts and banquets are organized here. The dishes served on these occasions include roast beef and pork, roast bacon, stuffed fish, as well as grilled dishes.
There is also a selection of excellent vegetarian dishes.

Polskie Smaki – ul. Św. Tomasza 5
You can start feasting here even in the morning, as the restaurant offers a variety of breakfast dishes. There are also soups, such as "zhur" (a kind of rye soup), red "borsch" and tomato soup. The main course may consist of stuffed cabbage rolls, pork chops, minced cutlets, pancakes, pork knuckles and many other delicacies.

Gościniec – ul. Stradomska 11
The place boasts excellent "pierogi", pork, beef and poultry dishes. The restaurant advertises them as prepared using the highest quality ingredients and traditional Polish recipes. The restaurant also offers its own cakes and a large variety of coffees and teas.

Mieszczańska – ul. Zwierzyniecka 29
This is a restaurant offering a wide range of typically Polish dishes including starters, soups, "pierogi" and meat dishes. The prices are very reasonable. The restaurant has also prepared a surprise for its guests. It is a culinary map of Krakow, which is a selection of dishes traditionally associated with the trendiest places in this city. They are certainly worth trying.

Table of contents